A Day in My Shoes

If You Don't Stand For Something Then You'll Fall For Anything

Authored By:
Cash • Lex • Rae • Muffin • C.I.V. • Dee • Mini
Smiley • Sosaa • Momo • Faith • Panda •1K
That Girl• Unknown • Charlie 5k • L.A. Rhea• I'm V
V.S. Kountry • Harmonic Virtue

A Day in My Shoes: *If You Don't Stand For Something Then You'll Fall For Anything*

Written by anonymous female students June 2017.

Published by:
Affirmative Expression
PO Box 360856
Decatur, GA 30036

First edition copyright © 2017, Affirmative Expression

All rights reserved. No part of this book may be reproduced or transmitted in any form or by any means, electronic or mechanical, including photocopying, recording, or by any information storage or retrieval system, without written permission of the author.

Cover by Chelsey Thomas
chels.t14@gmail.com

Printed in the United States of America

ISBN: **978-0-9963605-7-9**

A Day in My Shoes

Letter from the Publisher

The Anthology Project is a program created to provide a platform for voices to be heard. Often times youth feel their voices are not valuable. Others may feel pressure from the concern of their work being good enough for a passing grade. But while participating in this collaborative project they are able to speak freely with no concern for whether they will pass or fail. Most importantly, through the support of readers like you, their voices, stories, and efforts are validated and for that I thank you.

Tierica Berry
CEO
A Woman's Standard

FOREWORD

When I created the Anthology Project it was to shed light on the voice of today's youth as it relates to various topics. Over the past few months I have had the honor and pleasure of working with these student authors to create this work of art.

These young ladies were asked about managing emotions. During dialogue about the issues teens face trying to manage their emotions they were able to share their stories as well as the stories of others together and write this book:

A Day in My Shoes
If You Don't Stand For Something You'll Fall For Anything

Take your time and experience the journey as these talented authors show you A Day in their shoes.

Enjoy.

♥

Tierica Berry

CONTENTS

1 Teens and Emotions 9

2 The Importance 31

3 Emotional Triggers 35

4 Advice 57

To the Girls,

Life has a way of polishing you as well as bruising you; uplifting and impelling you, as well as restraining and circumscribing you.

Through it all, you must learn to pray, forgive, love, meditate and truly live; express gratitude, compassion, sympathy or empathy. Watch your words and actions beforehand because once it's spoken or done, you cannot take either one back. Every decision in life yields a consequence whether it is good or bad. And every new day brings new opportunities.

We all have different battles, the difference is in how we respond or deal with them. Do not allow your actions in your teen years to negatively affect the rest of your adult years. Negatively formed thoughts and atrocious attitudes creates dysfunctional lives and emotionally battered people.

Our bodies are mystifying, our emotions complex. Emotions can be affected by numerous entities including our environment, experiences, chemical imbalances, as well as our thoughts alone. Emotions play a large role in our ability to succeed or fail when facing the challenges of life. As your life progresses and you mature into productive, responsible adults in society, always make positive affirmations about yourself and over your life. You may feel the pains of the past but you are not the hurt of your past. Do not let the pains of the past define who you become. Create that one big dream, EDUCATE yourself, and don't stop, keep moving. Nobody can do everything but everybody can do something.

Keep moving.
Respectfully written,
Ms. K. T. Parker

CHAPTER 1

Teens and Emotions

*The authors were asked,
"Why do some teenagers have a hard
time managing their emotions?"*

André

My brother, I looked up to him

Now he up the road doin time

He taught me right from wrong

Left from right

All that good stuff

Taught me how to be a lady,

Even though he's a man

Taught me how to hold myself together

How to rep, he's my right hand

I'm that young soldier

He's my O.G.

"Through the eyes of the Warrior, Up Top?"

He always said to me, I would say

"Through the sword of the Warlord,

D.O.A I love my Billies more"

I looked up to him

Wanted to be him

Nobody was real but him

It hurts, I really have no one

Even though it looks like I do

A Day in My Shoes

I don't, not like he was

Lowkey my whole life is through

I ask myself

"Who am I now?"

I am confused but he would've helped

figure the answer out if he could

My brother, I looked up to him

Now he up the road doin LIFE!

-Sosaa

IM STILL ALIVE.

Young girl who made many mistakes

She didn't care about the consequences she would have to face

So she stayed stuck in one place

She didn't believe she could run the good race

Her life was filled with hopeless aspirations

Because she chased life's temptations

She was fast & furious

She was always so curious

Playing Life like tic tack toe

she couldn't get her X's & O's in the right rows

She hid her hurts and pain because it was so deep that it overflowed

Living a life of crime became a continued episode

She was so blind to her pain that even if it rained she could not see her scars

So being locked away was now her fate, and her dreams no longer were shooting stars

She discovered that inside she was growing a new seed

How was she to succeed?

Into His heart she began to swim

He gave her a new hope

He told her that even though you made mistakes, I will still give you a clean slate

You are not dead

So Daughter of mine lift up your head

A Day in My Shoes

Look to me for all your needs

I will help you fulfill all your dreams

Daughter I heard your screams

Now is the time to believe

You can change your life, with me this is something you can achieve

Your daughter is not a curse, she is your blessing

So you no longer have to keep guessing

Become alive

Because you will survive

I stood up

And said

I was the young girl who made many mistakes

I didn't know what doing right would take

But I stand here and say

That I am Still Alive

-**Unknown**

I Did It

Yeah, I did it

I hit "licks"

I did drugs

I even got a couple of bills

But what's the point?

I had to get it how I lived

Raised by a mother and father, so why did I steal? She got this, he got that

But what did I have? How did they live?

Made my first stack of money and got robbed the same night. It's funny because I knew them. But damn, I was just a kid

"Go to school Smiley that's how you'll live" my mama said. But I just wanted to hit for mills

I wanted to eat... to help pay bills. So I learned how drive, every time you'd see me I was behind a wheel. So I did crimes. Yeah, and the time. All I knew was the system took my father. Cold world, cold heart. I had to learn how to stick and move and play my part. I remember being flipped. I got told on, crazy because it was with people I'd never fold on. Stuck in a hole. Mama was hurt. She just didn't know her daughter turned cold. So there I was, stuck in a jail cell. Until one Tuesday night a lady from a church program came and communicated with me. She gave me a key. The key was God. I accepted him into my heart. All he said was "play your part" it was hard but I made it. I realized my emotions held me back. The whole time I was being stabbed in the back. The streets never loved me I had a family waiting for me. I had people waiting who loved me. So yeah, been there done that and made it through that. So yeah, I did it

-Smiley

Bless

Been through a lot got touch on and abuse

Been to jail wondering in life why I was so confuse

Sense I was 8 try to jump out the window

My soul was dark my mind was black

Now I'm facing 20 years my heart got crack

This is me a bless girl that never go to deep

My heart was racing when she touch on me

Call it a curse or a blessing

My life was bad and good it was all a lesson

Jesus told me to chin up or the crown well slip

So I did what I had to do and pull a grip

They say count your blessing and I had a lot

Words that Dee gave me I tied them into a knot

The devil try to snatch me up but he forgot I was bless

He never know what Jesus plan for me so he pay attention to the next

I'm wise I'm confuse I'm beautiful and sweet

My past was a nightmare but that was a beginning for me

I'm bless! I'm bless!

Nothing more nothing less.

-Mini

A Day in My Shoes

"Past"

Basketball used to be my life,

Drugs and money changed my mind,

Things quickly changed over time

I use to come home and see my mother cry.

I remember shooting balls in the hoop,

Then I got my first gun and was ready to shoot,

Surrounded by OGs that speak the truth,

But I hated being told what to do.

Momma taught me how to have respect,

It still didn't stop me from getting a check,

Momma screaming at me "come in the house",

If I talked back she'll pop me in the mouth.

I really missed playing on the court,

Now I'm staring at the judge sitting in court,

I was just a toddler playing with play-dough

Now I'm playing with guns like a game of Halo.

Don't blame my mom this is not the way she made me,

I made my mistakes now I'm asking God to please save me!

-Dee.

Misunderstood

People say I ain't never going to change. People say I'd amount to nothing. If I change I got to exchange. That's not me. That's not who I want to be. It takes a lot of strength in me to be who I don't want to be. People judge me people try to cover me I'm praying for change I'm trying, but it's still not enough, it's not normal that I hold in a lot of stuff. Surrounded by hypocrites who tell me to do right but they're not living a regular life. Trying to find love in all the wrong places, I can't even get it on regular basis. They say no to drugs but I smoke a blunt to hide all these faces. To unknown people I keep facing. I got faith I'm gone live to see another day. Still misunderstood and trapped in all the wrong places. My family expects me to change overnight, but a person like me, all I know is crime. How can I change overnight. How can you just wake up one morning and quit something that you are addicted too. It's impossible unless you are God. Someone who's in love with smoking weed. How can they wake up one morning and say I'm addiction free. All the rehab in the world can't help you unless you want to be free. I choose the life of crime to find a family because I don't

A Day in My Shoes

feel like I belong in my family. My family never understood why I choose the life of a criminal cause I never really felt like I had a family. I was raped by my brother when I was 9. My heart ran away because nobody believed me. Lost in a cold world by myself. Dad nowhere to be found. Mom in and out of hospitals trying to get her mind right. After 17 years of living, she is just now learning how to be a mom. No one understands why I do what I do. I'm just trying to make it out here in these streets. Just now finding myself after running in these streets since I was just a little kid. I remember as a kid getting the TV cut off because we couldn't pay the bill. Life wasn't always that bad growing up. Still misunderstood trying to find a way out the hood.

By. Panda

Teenagers have a hard time managing emotions because people don't experience what they experience. Other people don't know how to hold in things for so long. Look, imagine sitting in a dark bathroom crying. Or just stuck in your thoughts in a dark bathroom trying to hold everything in. My mother always told me "Life is meant to be difficult, remember Heaven is not earth". I was so stuck on my past life I never realized I had a whole life ahead of me. I did bad things out of anger. Emotions so deep that trouble surrounded them. I always knew right from wrong, but I was so hurt and filled with anger. I felt like the system took away my father, so I was angry. I felt like God took away my Aunt and Grandmother, so I was hurt. I knew bad things would make people upset. I wanted them to feel how I felt. I felt like I had no one but my mother. I needed something... No someone. I needed my father. I felt like God let me down. I was going down a bad road. But that bad road was something God was preparing me for. I never realized until I went to jail. A lady from a church program came to see me. I changed my whole mindset... This was real life. So that same night I went into my cell and poured everything out to God. All I asked for was peace and to be able to sleep better. I promise I was able to sleep good that same night for the first time in a long time. I got

released and stopped doing crimes. I changed all of my horrible ways. I started communicating with my father. All he wanted was for his daughter to stay out of trouble and make it in life. Till this day......
That's what motivates me.

- Smiley

A's

THEY SAY GO TO SCHOOL AND GET A'S FIND A GOOD JOB THAT PAYS

BUT HITTIN LICKS AND MOVIN BRICKS, UPPED MY WEIGHT

WHEN I WAS SKINNY, AIN'T HAD NOTHING ON MY PLATE

SCARS ON MY BACK LIKE I'VE BEEN THROUGH A HURRICANE…AND BACK

TEACHER'S DON'T HAVE NOTHING TO SAY ABOUT THAT

WAS QUICK TO CALL ME A HOOD RAT

TEACHERS TOUCHED ON ME BUT MADE SURE I PASSED

SO SCHOOL BECAME AN IN AND OUT TYPE THING

ONLY CAME WHEN I HAD CRANK TO SLANG OR B'S TO BANG

OTHER THAN THAT THE STREETS BECAME MY MAIN

MADE ME SMART, HAD ME GROWN FROM THE START

SEEMS LIKE I ALWAYS HAD A CHOICE TO MAKE, BUT THE STREETS WON AT THE END OF THE DAY

BECAUSE I DIDN'T WANT TO PAY THE PRICE THAT CAME WITH THE A'S

C.I.V

A Day in My Shoes

YOU KNOW THINGS ARENT ALWAYS EASY 5K

It's hard to keep going when you have no one; I understand, cause people aren't always jolly

Depression is a drug; I know all about it I just want the best; so I can make it out it 💯 Living in poverty, got exposed to drugs was looking for love; now I'm stuck with a thug; BOOM BOOM what's love. Now-a-days these dudes want nothing but Neck nothing more nothing less.

As young ladies become so thrilled to satisfy these men; we tend to forget where we even begin. Days have passed; week seem to fly. I just want to manage my emotions what about you? It's going to be hard to break through to be you & do you.

Maintain the whole way they gone HATE to see you

Just remember God loves you!!

I WON'T TELL YOU ANYTHING I HAVENT BEEN THROUGH

Charlie5k

(Chapter 1)

Why do you think some teenagers have a hard managing emotions?

In the poem you are about to read it will explain a mothers' pain soon after her young son passed away. This poem was written in dedication to my significant others' brother whom passed away during the time we were locked away from the world and were forced to face the grieving process as raw as it comes. My goal in this poem is to provide you with an inspiring life event that not only tore apart hearts but brought a family closer together.

Title: A mother's pain

Silent whimpers in making... One after another fatal organs start taking. Taking everything that once obtained life, spilling its sorrows and disrupting memories into many restless nights.

The closet hid her tears from the remaining children.... Too numb to face it in public, too done trying to be the best mother possible because when her boy slipped away he faded into the unstoppable. She held on tight but wanted so dearly to take his pain... "Go ahead, it's his time, it came!"

A drastic call called for more than life's measures. It amounted out to be 'weightless.' Weighing less than wondrous weathers... Whether it be the depression to follow or the abnormality to swallow. We'd just come to know what we had and where we got it, why we had it so little and how precious we saw it.

We all live amongst the dead and grieve through the living... Mourning in black, learning thanks "THANKSGIVING!" Teaching our children of two separate roads," The right and the wrong," but who really

A Day in My Shoes

knows? Teaching a ten year old how to ride a bike then the very next day he fights for his life.

Face swelling.... SWOLE! Tummy grumbling... HOLE!

Full of disease nowhere close to ease. Medicine pumping through every vein hoping to quickly subside his pain. His mother cry's out to the Lord "PLEASE GOD PLEASE, HE CAN'T TAKE IT ANYMORE!"

Slipping into absence, the best call was made. The Lord took her baby and vanished his earthly pain.

That same little boy owns a mansion in heaven and sacredly angels over the "7." Seven siblings at bond six living on. His story is incredibly beautiful and it lives forever on.

Rest in peace, little man.

We never got to meet, but I know you well enough to know that I am love you and you will reside in my heart forever. I am moved by your story and I hope to see you one day and that gorgeous mansion of yours.

- L.A. RHEA

(I'd like to add that grieving isn't always an easy thing to overcome but with the support and love of other people it makes that journey a much easier process. In this poem I based the story off of the pain of the child's mother because as a mother myself it was easier to relate. The child's sister and I actually came up with ways to cope and move forward shortly after his passing and I will include more of those skills in the following chapters. I will also be writing about ways people think and tend to feel during a time of hopelessness and ways they recover themselves and rehabilitate their minds from harsh feelings in themselves.)

"Why do children suffer from behavioral problems?"

"You're Pow"

Children and young adults suffer from behavioral problems for many reasons,

Sometimes even ending in different treasons.

What happens to kids in their past,

Will usually make these behavioral problems last.

We can have these problems,

From past reports of trauma.

Being neglected isn't fun,

It's like being away from the sun.

Physical abuse is even worse,

It's almost like being under a curse.

Emotional abuse hurts the most,

It's like your mind is on a roast.

Unfortunately children suffer way too much,

Your heart feels like it's under a hunch.

Luckily there's ways to feel better,

And it doesn't require writing a letter.

A Day in My Shoes

In the end it's up to you,

For what you really want to do.

You can end your behavioral problems now,

But it all starts with your POW.

-FAITH

They Judge Me

They all want to judge me
They see a blue bandana and think of gang
I see one and think of family
You see juveniles stealing, killing being criminals
I laugh and shrug my shoulders thinking that's just the way it is
As children we either follow in our parents footprints or we create our own
And when mom has suspicious guest over and my younger sister is crying from the discomfort
And from old soiled diaper, and food aint there, lights aint on
Whose gonna show a girl like me the right footsteps to walk in?
Whose gonna give a minority like me a job with my background
They all want to judge me
They heard an accent and think immigrant
I heard one and think nothing of it
I see an opportunity
I took it because when darkness is all you know you think to yourself what's so good about the light?
When racism is all you know, you ask why is it better than being white?
When blue is all you know, you never question why you hate red
As long as an OG gets you fed, an education is out of your head
They all want to judge me
Want to judge my shoes, but don't have the balls to step in them
they all want to tell me how it should be or how it could be
but I'm looking at my own struggle that sits in my face everyday
every other kid had a chance to have fun and live
a life where they had a say
I don't play with dolls or dream of things
I hit licks and make money
So maybe one day I can pay for a meal
Instead of daily rice and beans
So they all want to judge me now
My hurdle wasn't they way it should be
Well maybe if life was a little more fair and gave me a chance then it could be
So until that day when I'm not being followed in the streets by a perverted man

A Day in My Shoes

Until that day I can wake up one morning with a real air conditioner,
instead of a beat down fan
Then you can judge me

$$--\text{I'M V}$$

Momma

On the streets since I was nine
Lucky and surprised I haven't died
I've hit licks I've moved drugs
I've been considered a thug
Momma don't want me, daddy won't hurt me
What can I consider love?
Can't go down the street without my strap
I've learned to keep a close eye and watch my back
I was blessed into a gang, got kicked out the house
I remember sleeping next to a friendly mouse
Couldn't turn to the gang, I couldn't turn to my momma
All I could do is think about my past trauma
I ran up a check, wondering when will I earn my respect
Praying that the police won't break my neck
I come from the bottom to the top
But I can't stop to feel I'm being followed by a cop
I can't cry and I won't cry
Sometimes I wish I could fly
I've been in this game so long I always win
I strongly feel like daddy is the outside looking in
One day momma beat me, and all I heard were the neighbors yelling free me
To this day I have no contact with my mom
And it hurts real bad, like a plane full of bombs
She needed money so I stole cars
That's too bad she couldn't be then
I was facing life behind bars
So blood really ain't thicker than water
Cause me and moms is like oil and water
So if you ask me blood doesn't make a family
Momma just mad cause she couldn't handle me.

--I'M V

CHAPTER 2

The Importance

The authors were asked, "Whether they thing it is important t be able to manage their emotions?"

"Monster"

People are quick to judge me by my looks,

But they don't know I'm smart in the books,

I believe in blessings don't believe in luck,

I've been in situations where I sometimes felt stuck.

Take off my shirt and beat on my chest,

Screaming I want more, stop giving me less!

God said "Keep going this is not the end",

But God if I go, will I ever win?

Momma did drugs it did change a lot,

Wiping my tears along with the snot,

I am human but the other side is a monster,

Fighting to make it out of the jungle.

                                                                  -DEE

A Day in My Shoes

LUL SOULJAH

Learning to manage your emotions is good to know; it's hard when you came out the Dope Hole

And nowhere to go

There once was a girl who self-esteem was low

She had to shake back and get on her 10 toes

CHARLIE CHARLIE,

Remember you deserve more

Home getting crazy I gotta let that go

I just want a better hustle flow

And achieve a little more

People pray on your down fall

Just remain tall

RIP MY LIL DAWG

Fly high and you better touch **Jesus Christ** sky  AMEN!

Charlie5k

CHAPTER 3
Emotional Triggers

This chapter is a compilations of stories and examples of emotional triggers.

That Girl

Hands on my body they made me feel grown.

I was out all nights never coming home.

They all called me fast without knowing my past.

They all called me that girl

The girl you can count on when you're all alone

Yeah I guess you could say they called me grown

But one thing they didn't know is, I was lying in bed one night

He came in my room and I tried to put up a fight

But that night what he did to me wasn't right

They all called me that girl

The white girl who was from the projects

No I wasn't perfect

I had to hustle and stay on my grind

Never about what could happen to me stayed on my mind

They all called me that girl

The jailbird

I was only 12 when I started getting in trouble now I'm 16 and still locked up

All this just because I wanted love

They all knew my name

A Day in My Shoes

It wasn't fair game

But now I learned my lesson and I know to never be that girl again

-That Cordial Gurl-

In Just a Blink of an Eye

Approaching footsteps

There they go, I hear

BANG BANG BANG

Gunshots

Sirens All I Hear

Red and blue lights all I see

Area lit up like a Christmas tree

People running, screaming of murder

My world stands still

As I take it all in

My sight becomes a blur

My mind and body in shock

Watching everything around me crumble

In just a Blink of an Eye

My body became heavy

Dropped to my knees as I looked over

And seen my brother laying there

Motionless, Soulless

"Dead on Scene!"

Officer yelled

A Day in My Shoes

My best friend was dead

In just a Blink of an Eye

-V.S.KOUNTRY

In Loving Memory Of

C.T.W.

06.04.96 – 05.22.16

Untitled

Screeches from the tires on the road

No sirens in the distance,

Maybe 'cause nobody called

POP POP POP

My brothers down on the floor

He leakin, red seepin from him

Them other hittas, they run

Screeches from the tires on the road

They comin back

Grab my fye and I cock it

Ready to bust it back

POP POP POP

My sister down on the floor

Brains seepin from her head

I can't bare to look anymore

I'm poppin and bustin caps 'till

I can't bust anymore

They gone

In the distance

Screeches from the tires on the road

A Day in My Shoes

I pull them both into the whip

Knowing one is already gone

I tell my brother to be strong

He's losing too much red

I can't lose him, that would be wrong

Speeding to the ER

Screeches from the tires on the road

- Sosaa

I Want To Go Home

By: Cash

Free

Me…

A Day in My Shoes

My Truth

Grew up without a father

It made me grind harder

Fell in love with the streets

Doing anything for a dollar

In the lanes is where I would be

Could never catch me without my heat

But I'm in a cell

Praying not to go to hell

By: *1k*

Best friend

We started off as friends then it quickly became more than that.

The first day I saw you; I said, "This is going be fun getting to know you."

Never knew how wonderful you were until I started dreaming.

Now I think I'm in love with you. Hope I'm not dreaming.

I'm in a 6 by 9 cell and I can't see you. I'm not going crazy but I really miss you.

We are good together I know you see that. Why won't you go out with me?

Best friend, best friend why can't we be. I hope it's not your mother telling you that we can't be.

By. Panda

A Day in My Shoes

Trying to survive

I been thuggin since a jit

Doing anything just to hit

Hitting licks, flipping bricks

Doing anything just to hit

Robbing with a stick

That's holding a 30 clip

Cooling with my hittas,

Just trynna make a check flip…

By: 1K

MAY 8th

With my head over the rail, yelling "yeah I'm tryna come!"

That was the last thing I said to him before my world was spun

There was no sound, so quiet you could hear my heart pound

My senses were gone

Didn't know if he was dead or not because I was young

I ran so fast I could've got a scholarship for track

So much blood I could a started a drive

He was dead, I couldn't believe what was in front of my eyes

Standing there in just socks, underwear, and a bandana.

I took off my clothes to tie around his wounds so he could get better

Got it together, wiped my eyes and I started dragging him

Maybe I could make it to the hospital in time

My cousin pulled up told me to put it to rest, there was no use he was dead

I didn't realize what was said til I seen that sheet over his head, with his eyes closed, with no beat in his chest

My brother the only one that cared, especially every time my momma disappeared

My protector, wiped my tears, held me through my nightmares

Told all those men about themselves who have touched me all those years

What am I going to do? I love and need him more than anything out hear.

Now I'm lost, scared and confused.

Well, it's present day and God has taken many things since May 8th

Four other brothers, three sisters, my cousin and my uncle

A Day in My Shoes

And its messed me up in every way

But ever since may 8th I haven't been able to feel anything anyway

I can't control my anger because I never got closer, he was killed in front of my face

Didn't get a chance to say what I needed to say to feel okay

So now I got pressure on my chest and my mind never sleeps

But now I pray every day and just ask god to give my heart peace and let my mind sleep

-C.I.V

PASSION

Our passion is so vivid.

It's so good that it's so hard to let go.

When we are together magical things happen.

Your tenderness to love is my weakness to your heart.

I yearn for your love because your love is so bright.

Sweetheart you're going to be mine tonight.

Be in love with me for just one night.

Have weakness for desert tonight while we make love in are passion tonight.

By. Panda

A Day in My Shoes

"Age is just a number"

Daddy over dosed me at 2 years old, left me in a coma for 9 weeks whole.

I left the projects at age three, into a home for half the fee.

I ended up moving in with my momma, her new boyfriend was full of drama.

At one point he made me chew glass, it showed me his major lack of class.

My body all bruised was nothing new, but I stuck to myself like I was glue.

It was only when I was four, that I thought I wouldn't be anything more.

They finally broke up so I thought the abuse would stop, but just then I realized something new about to make me pop.

We moved down to Florida without any luck, with barely anything to spare not even a buck.

My momma had a new husband who thought he was fly, but he always made me feel like I wanted to die.

At five I noticed something new ahead, when my mom was always sick in bed.

A few months later my mom had a baby, I asked if it was a boy and she said "maybe".

Her and my step dad loved that kid, enough to put me up for bid.

As the years went by I got more scars and cuts, I felt like I was pretty much just a mutt.

At seven years old my other brother was born, but I realized everyone was starting to mourn.

My parents were both really bad drunks, I always tried hiding in my bunk.

The look in my eyes showed the pain. I had plenty of time just to gain.

At the age of seven, the rape had started, and I had felt completely parted.

I always felt gross, and was ready for the roast.

When I was 10 I had a best pone, he was 80 years old in a nursing home.

When I visited him he had a stroke, which ended in me taking a toke.

I went on my own to find a nurse, but he took a turn for the worse.

My friend had died right in front of my face, my eyes turned watery like I was sprayed with mace.

When I was 14, I'd had enough. I decided to become abrupt.

I ended up dropping out of school. I low key started acting like a fool.

I started doing every drug in the book, and acting like a complete crook.

My boyfriend and I moved into his home, I thought of it like my own little dome.

Everything felt great until up to this time, when I heard the front bell go off like a chime.

He was always hitting me and making me cry, making me think I should lie.

When I was 15, I was 6 months pregnant, but then I realized something.

He came home on a mere, then I was the evil in him wasn't pure.

He hurt me bad enough to make me lose my child, which was part of the reason I went wild.

A few months later when everything was calm and steady, I got some news in which I wasn't ready.

I found out my step grandma had suffered a tragic death, my way of dealing with it was when I slept.

She was pushed off her balcony in Ohio, by her own autistic child.

This loss affected me in various ways, I felt alone for many days.

A Day in My Shoes

When I turned 16, I caught a charge, my consequences were very large.

They took my charge a lot further, and ended up turning it into murder.

I prayed to God day and night, I was always full of fright.

In jail I finally became drug free, people stopped feeling bad for me.

I got out after about a month, I felt like the pressure was a ton.

Then I made another mistake, and returned back to the slammer feeling fake.

I caught over 15 charges, praying to God for special bargains.

The courts told me I had to serve 20 years, right from then I could feel the tears.

I finally made a big decision, and prayed to God for a revision.

He ended up hearing my prayer, I got a shorter sentence later.

I used to hit liqs all the time, leaving people on the ground like a lime.

I took lots of drugs and was never sober, I was lucky to be alive kind of like a four leaf clover.

I turned my self around and acted like this never took place, it's just a bump in the road and it's time to tie the lace.

But the only thing that could help my mistakes, and the steps I decided to take.

With big goals ahead of me and many dreams to follow too, I want to help kids in the same position that I led myself into.

But with happiness to come; don't worry about the past, put it all aside and make good decisions last.

They say I should take my own advice but at the end of each day, I see myself growing with progress so my new potential does stay.

In a few years I plan on studying law, helping those like me who have gone through it all.

-Faith

A Day in My Shoes

How About Dattt

Imagine getting shot to the brain;

Your mind goes blank and you feel insane!

Being emotionally triggered is no game

But everybody don't feel the same

I know **LEX** know how to maintain

Sometimes she play games like Fun Brain

But back to the real thing

Some say life is a game

That's why society views us as a shame

How about dattt

-Charlie5k

"What is an emotional trigger?"

"Results"

What is an emotional trigger, you may ask? Let's start off by how they're caused. Emotional triggers are caused by anything traumatizing or mournful that have happened to you whether recent or long ago. Death or breaking up with a spouse, anything that brings up bad memories or emotions from the past is considered an emotional trigger.

When being emotionally triggered, you're thinking about these unhappy events that may have severely impacted you. You may have flashbacks or suffer from PTSD as a result. Other side effects are crying and self-harming.

Being impacted emotionally has severe consequences. Being emotionally triggered is one memory coming back and replaying in your head over and over again.

Being emotionally triggered is the one feeling that feels like nothing will be the same.

What is most important about being emotionally triggered is over coming it... the way I was able to...

-FAITH

A Day in My Shoes

FLASHBACKS

I fell asleep, I see him in my dreams
Like Freddy Kruger he keeps appearing
I wonder will he ever leave me
He opens my door, he comes in closer
He lays on me, we're like two breads in a toaster
He touches my body, he kisses my neck
I can't stop to wonder, "What the heck?"
Two years go by, now I'm nine
Momma beat me so hard I thought I died
Younger sister, older brother, and I are in foster care
I wonder if this old man will ever disappear
I begged my dad to come get me out this place
While that old man kisses under my waist
A couple of months go by when I first got high
I rolled my blunt I crushed my weed
I thought this is just what I need
A little weed turned into a pill
A pill turned into three or four pills
While I stole daddy's money for pills, he struggled to pay his bills
I woke up
Years later I'm seventeen, praying to God to see eighteen
I've run the streets now I'm here
I don't regret shhh cause it was dear
I thank God my dad is straight, I feel he's near
But I can't stop these flashbacks
Back to my old tears

-I'm V

CHAPTER 4

Advice

Lastly, the authors were asked to share some advice about managing emotions.

"HUMBLE"

They ask me how I let my talent go to waste,

I responded quickly, "life got in the way",

Curled up like a ball and my stomach feeling empty,

I am no kill but these people, they tempt me.

I got the heart of a lion, with the soul of a tiger,

With a body of ninja, and a brain of a fighter,

I stay away from the people that are supposed to be "friends",

Cause those are the ones who are going to change in the end.

Momma always told me that life is precious, but hard,

I should've listened to momma and kept up my guard,

My daddy was sentenced to life when I was five,

Kind of glad I faced hard times because I am now wise.

Sitting in a room where I could hear my heart beat,

A Day in My Shoes

My life is like the ocean it gets really deep,

I am that kid who is always in trouble,

But I'm also that kid that always stay humble.

-Dee.

Love is blind

Love is so blind that I can barely see the light.

I never knew how blind I was till it hit me in the eye.

It was so crazy because I thought we were in love.

I used to think that was love until I had enough.

Now I don't know who to trust; it's never enough.

Love is a battle but my compassion is always too much.

I never knew she could be so cruel.

Now I can finally say that I found my way out of this dark hole we call love.

By. Panda

Dedicated to my little sister, "Catie."

A Day in My Shoes

WHITE

It's like laying on a cloud like you could do anything

But the feelings is so good it's almost like you already accomplished everything

Wasn't angry no more, wasn't sad no longer

Could face the world head on and handle my problems

I loved the feeling of being in control, thinking I knew in life exactly where I wanted to go

Snow, yay, yayo or whatever your hood calls it had me feelin like I was king of everything

Cocaine, that one little line, had me feelin like I could do anything and everything

But this wasn't reality, it tricked me

Cause when I came down my momma still didn't love me, my brother was still six feet under and I was still hungry

So what did that hit really do for me?

Cause after that quick 30, I still remembered my pain and everyone that hurt me

But I still appreciate it in a strange way

Even though I'm off it in present day

Because it gave me an escape

Something I needed to be sane

Not knowing at 12 it wasn't the right way

Since I know now, I'll stay far away

Because fool me once shame on you

I'm not going to let you fool me twice because that'll be shame on me…

C.I.V

A Day in My Shoes

Made for it

Help is hard to ask for so I walk light, just trying to do good and doing what is right

You can't help someone who doesn't want to be helped!

Now-a-days everybody getting killed on that hot life

And handling it with that act right

Keep your head up big bruh just chill

GANK GANNK

I had to buckle down but; I'm trying to touch **a Mill**

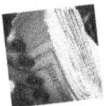

Remember to keep it real and say how you feel!

Learn to manage your emotions without them pills

And that's for real though

Charlie5k

My Soul to Take

Not one day goes by that I don't think of that day
Not one day goes by without this fake smile on my face
I just don't understand
I swear, every night I hit my knees and pray
And I know you feel my pain because you made me this way
So God I ask you to help me day by day
So I can be able to make my way
All this pain I keep it in
I stay wondering if I'll ever win
I've run the streets, I've made my way
I pray the Lord my soul to take
Only he knows how it goes
Round and round the same old road
In and out of jail
Wondering if this is just a tale
A tale with no happy ending, I begin repenting
It s turning my life into a nightmare
A nightmare as long as a light year
Years after years I push further away
But I continue to pray the Lord my soul to take.

--I'M V

A Day in My Shoes

Destiny

Lord, it is in Your hands,

Let Your will be done.

May You give me strength to endure and emerge from it all.

Lord, it is in Your hands,

I have faith in You, and You alone.

For I continuously praise and give thanks unto Your Holy Name.

Praying, trusting the process, and relying on Your unmerited favor.

My destiny.

For what has been, is, and will be,

Lord, it is in Your hands,

The Only One who remains faithful, consistent, and true.

Harmonic Virtue

EMERGING

From the infinite flow of tears for so many years,

EMERGING

From love lost;

smothered emotions and expectations of perfection,

EMERGING

From nights of cold sweats, dreams of falling,

running in complete darkness,

EMERGING

From self-inflicted hate, pain and confusion

caused when allowing society to define me,

EMERGING

Beautiful Black Queen,

Formed from the pressures of this world

Just as a diamond in the mines or a pearl in the great blue seas,

EMERGING

Harmonic Virtue

A DAY IN *YOUR* SHOES

Now that you have walked a day in our shoes, it's time for you to document your own journey. The following pages are to help you get started. Maybe you can use the stories you write here to get started on your own book! ;-)

A Day in My Shoes

Affirmative expression would like to congratulate these contributing authors for completing
The Anthology Project

and earning the prestigious title of
published authors!

If you would like to bring **The Anthology Project** to your school, church, program, or organization please contact us!

Affirmative Expression's
Anthology Project
Turning your students into authorpreneurs!
Tierica Berry (Founder)
678.499.4405
Info@AffirmativeExpression.com
www.AffirmativeExpression.com

www.ingramcontent.com/pod-product-compliance
Lightning Source LLC
Chambersburg PA
CBHW071751040426
42446CB00012B/2523